FAM OUS IN TERI ORS

THE ORIGINALS

FAM OUS IN TERI ORS

THE ORIGINALS

CONCEPT PHOTOGRAPHY STYLING
Holland Vandertol
TEXT   DESIGN
Cornelia van Gelder   **Borinka**

TERRA

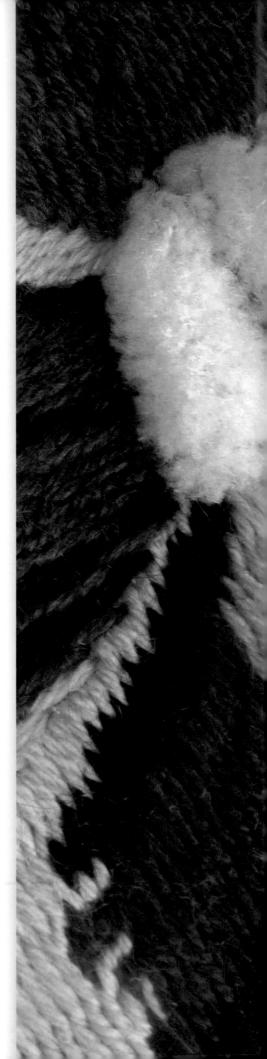

■■■■■ with special thanks to

The originals who had the nerve to throw open their doors.
Jason Kontos of New York Spaces for the preface.
Bert Zuiderveen for processing the images.
Gigia and **Claudio Marchiori**, my agents in New York,
for their assistance in preparing this book.
Cornelia van Gelder for her enthusiastic texts.
Borinka for her refreshing design.
Arie Dekker for his moral support and legal guidance.
Paul Mosterd for his good advice.
Marieke van Gessel, journalist, for originating the contact
with the Missonis and The People of the Labyrinths.
Craig Delos Seebach, without whom the step
toward photography would never have been taken.
Karin van der Tol and **Rob van Gameren**
for their personal support and constructive criticism.
Manon Heida, Lupe, **Fay** and **Juultje Tijink**
for their unrelenting enthusiasm.
Corinne Bensahel, Roland Hagenberg and **Dorothée van Hooff**

■■■■■ colophon

© **2008 Terra Lannoo Publishers B.V.**
P.O. Box 614 - 6800 AP Arnhem, The Netherlands
info@terralannoo.nl
www.terralannoo.nl
Terra Publishers is a part of the Lannoo Group, Belgium

© **2008 Holland Vandertol**
www.hollandvandertol.com

concept, photography and styling **Holland Vandertol**
text **Cornelia van Gelder**
design **Borinka**
english translation **Deul & Spanjaard, Groningen**
printing and binding **Printer Trento, Trento (Italy)**

The materials used for the cover are details from
the interiors of Michele Oka Doner (front cover),
the Kortmann family (back) and John Barman (spine).
The embroideries that adorn the introductory pages
were created by Erica Wilson.

ISBN Eng. 978-90-5897-986-5
ISBN Ned. 978-90-5897-877-6
NUR 454

contents

timeless personal interiors

██████████ Who is the owner of that remarkable steel shed in L.A.? Who resides immersed in art and an eclectic mix of collectables in a New York apartment? Who inhabits that modern home in Milan? To whom do they belong?

Holland Vandertol and Cornelia van Gelder escort you in. You enter the abode of no one less than actor Dennis Hopper, avant-garde designer Vladimir Kagan, the fashion designers Rosita and Ottavio Missoni, and other renowned names.

Is there anyone who doesn't become confused by all the demands that our interior design ought to meet – at least according to the shelter magazines and design themed television programs? Our homes and our belongings are dear to us. But, if we believe the media, it is of the utmost importance to change our homes rigorously every year, or at any rate restyle them.

It has to be continually different and above all perpetually new. Do we really desire that? Most lifestyle articles ignore the essence of living: our own place, one that harmonizes with who we are. Trendy decorating 'must haves' soon bore us (the neighbors have them too!) and they are soon up for replacement. This leads to financial squandering and mountains of unnecessary rubbish. And the question still remains: do we really feel at home in our home?

To demonstrate that it can all be done very differently, this book presents an anthology of personal interiors. The residents are all people from the world of art and design. These Originals have not only made their marks in their own professional fields, they all maintain a very personal view of the world and particularly of their own living environment. It is striking to observe just how well their interiors harmonize with their personalities and even appear to emphasize them.

The Originals do not participate in a servile pursuit of fashion crazes; they follow their own tastes. Their interiors are the result of a process lasting many years. In the course of time, their interiors have become 'richer', as more and more layers of significance are added, featuring acquisitions that embody memories and narratives. Things are rarely discarded. In contrast, items for which there is no space at one particular time are stored away … they may be recalled some day.

With this anthology, the attentive reader, and especially the viewer, has a sample card of styles at hand. This book wishes to be a source of inspiration in making durable choices for an interior in which the personality of the resident is more important that the umpteenth whim of fashion.

By consciously making our own choices, not only do we become weary of our own interiors much less quickly, but we also feel much more at ease in our own home. The Originals have paved the way and will guide us onward.

████████

JAMIE DRAKE

a modern Louis XIV in a soft-yellow Rolls-Royce

▬▬▬▬▬ Jamie Drake is currently one of America's most renowned and requested interior designers. From New York to San Francisco, from Minneapolis to Austin, he has made a deep impression on modern American celebrity lifestyle. Color, luxury and glamour are his trademarks. But Drake also has an outspoken feeling for style as well as exceptional taste. 'If I had to choose who I would like to be, I would opt for Louis XIV,' he once admitted.

Jamie Drake came to New York with Madonna many years ago. He converted her beach house in L.A. into such an attention-grabbing residence that the glossy mags were queuing up for articles and Drake quickly became a favored guest at parties organized by filmstars, popstars and fashion designers.

In 2004, Drake was proclaimed International Interior Designer of the Year. From that moment onward, no one could fail to take notice of his work. He soon received more prestigious assignments, with the renovation of Gracie Mansion, the official residence of New York Mayor Michael Bloomberg, as the provisional highlight of his career. 'It's not sufficient to offer clients a good interior. You have to give them a special bond by supplying a substantial dose of emotion and drama as well,' is his motto. Those who have been charmed by the flamboyant designer remain loyal to him. Drake even has a customer for whom he has completed nine different projects, including two airplanes, a helicopter, and a boat.

In the interior designer world, admiration for Drake's bold use of color has brought him the nickname 'Mister Color'. But Jamie Drake is a colorful character even in his private life. He dresses in elegant, colorful suits and drives around in a yellow Rolls Royce.

In his youth, Jamie Drake had a great penchant for drawing and coloring. Above all, he delighted in creating sketches of interiors, and his extraordinary feeling for bold color combinations was already evident. 'What fascinates me about color arrangements is the fact that they can strengthen a space,' he says, 'they can bring it to life and give it glamour. I really adore unusual colors, indeterminate tints that seem to change in shade depending on the incidence of light. And I enjoy combining colors in an almost gaudy way.'

Drake's own spacious apartment on Fifth Avenue in New York amply displays his passion for color and intense combinations. With bright pink, vibrant canary yellow, fashionable purple tints and a sparkling golden accent here and there, he has transformed a long narrow space into a spacious yet simultaneously intimate house. He has left the original details of the former piano showroom untouched. No doors have been installed in the space that was originally an office, but walls have been erected here and there to partition off some areas and to ensure privacy.

Despite the bold colors, Drake's interiors are never glaring but always tasteful. In the hall, he stylishly combines the bright-pink walls with a series of silk screens by the American artist Gene Davis and for the bedroom with its vivid yellow walls and curtains, he opts for eye-catching animal prints on the floor and bed.

Drake invariably knows how to introduce artworks into an interior in an aesthetic way. Occasionally, when furnishing a space,

he allows himself to be inspired by an object or work of art itself. The dining room is an excellent example. Here an enormous self-portrait of Chuck Close dominates the room. It seems as if the work of art has been specially created for the place where Drake has hung it but, in reality, the wall has been adapted to accommodate the painting.

Jamie Drake's style comes to full expression in the living room too: the blend of furniture styles makes it colorful, fashionable and theatrical. The relatively neutral space was hung with pleated curtains and the furniture itself was upholstered in pink and purple plush. In the middle of the room, a round ottoman, large enough to serve as a bed, is the focus of attention. It is a splendid example of the way in which Drake plays with proportion.

At the same time, Drake also regards tranquility in his interiors as being of the utmost importance. 'I warn customers who want to display lots of objects to be careful about doing so. Don't forget that your eyes must be able to find a certain serenity in a space. That is why I would never combine a strong background with a lively still life and numerous objects, but only with a well-chosen item of furniture or an appealing work of art.'

In the design of his apartment on Fifth Avenue, Drake has clearly made no concession whatsoever with regard to his personal taste. The result is exciting and powerful, yet elegant and controlled. The apartment also demonstrates his great feeling for fashion and an even greater feeling for drama. The fact that Drake feels akin to the charismatic King Louis XIV, whose marvellous sense of style made France legendary, is thus perhaps not so very surprising... ▬▬▬▬▬

◀ **living room** (p. 10-11)
The large pink ottoman serves as an eye-catcher. Behind the sofa, which is a design by Jamie Drake, there is a painting by the Argentinian painter Graciela Hasper. The gilded chair from Germany dates from the 19th century, as does the Persian carpet. The standard for the painting next to the sofa was produced by Fontana Arte and dates from the fifties.
The tables are by Lorin Marsh.

◀ **living room** (p. 13) The bronze clock is a replica of an artwork by Salvador Dali.

◀ **hall** A series of silk screens by Gene Davis dating from 1978. The table by Intrex dates from the seventies.

▶ **dining room** The painting is a self-portrait by Chuck Close.

JAMIE DRAKE 15

living room Painting by Lois Renzoni (top left).
The floor lamp was designed by Drake (bottom left).
The two armchairs are by Jean Michel Frank.
Just like the tables, they are also French and date
from the thirties (large photo).
White Italian pottery from the fifties, richly
decorated with gold leaf, adorns the coffee table.

bedroom The walls in the guestroom (bottom right)
are covered in Venetian stucco to mimic leather panels.
The French mirror from the forties is enclosed in a
jade frame. The nail pattern on the bed was designed
by Drake. Lamps by the American designer John
Thompson stand on the bedside tables, which Drake
inherited from his grandmother.

DENNIS HOPPER

the idiosyncratic fort
of an American buccaneer

██████ Paranoia is a significant theme in the life and work of Dennis Hopper. And that also applies to his residential situation. His house is a steel fort in which the garage doors are used more frequently than the front door. It is undoubtedly the only house in the world in which you have a chance of being run down by a car while you are quietly sitting watching television.

The name Dennis Hopper will always be connected to the American cult film Easy Rider, dating from 1969, or to his role as a psychopath in Blue Velvet from 1986. The fact that Hopper is also an exceptionally gifted photographer and artist is less well-known. Much has been written and said about Hopper. He is apparently regarded as the personification of the good and the bad from the sixties. In the meantime, Hopper has played in many of the most important films of the last five decades, and is one of Hollywood's most striking personalities.

After spending a lonely childhood in Kansas, young Dennis succeeded in breaking into Hollywood and played supporting roles in the James Dean films Rebel Without a Cause and Giant. It seemed to be the start of a glorious career, but Hopper's journey through life also encountered many lows. After the phenomenal success of Easy Rider, Hopper regularly struggled with alcohol and drugs. In the early eighties, Hopper got back on his feet again and made a glorious come-back with a role as a psychopath in the film Blue Velvet.

Hopper not only expresses himself as an actor and director, but also as a painter, sculptor and photographer. In addition, he also devotes time and energy to his magnificent art collection. Hopper sees himself not only as an artist but also as an art connoisseur. 'I already knew the work of Andy Warhol and Roy Lichtenstein before they even had their own exhibitions.'

Hopper is now married for the fifth time. As a direct consequence of his divorces, his pop-art collection has substantially diminished. 'At the time, I bought Andy Warhol's Campbell's Soup Tins for sixty dollars. Now one of my exes has it.' Despite the artworks he has lost, Hopper still owns an impressive collection of paintings, including work by Julian Schnabel, Keith Haring and Andy Warhol. In conjunction with his own paintings and photos, they form a major part of the interior of his house in Los Angeles.

Hopper's house is situated in the questionable neighborhood of Venice Beach, and it looks like an impregnable fort. A section of the house was designed by Frank Gehry (who also designed the Guggenheim Museum in Bilbao), while another part was designed by Brian Murphy. They made use of unusual materials such as steel plates, plywood, corrugated iron, wire mesh, glass and asphalt. The interior gives a disorienting effect as a consequence of the many angles and distorted lines, and the connections with steel stairways and bridges. The high space has minimal windows to the outside; light enters primarily via the roof and the inner courtyard. 'It is perfect light for my art collection,' states Hopper.

As far back as the seventies, master-architect Gehry was building houses with pre-fab elements and exploded sections. They had to give the impression that the house was self-constructed, unfinished and unstable. At first, Hopper bought only a loft

and hired Brian Murphy to create the layout. A few years later he had Murphy build an 'art gallery' as an annex, and he bought a second studio from Gehry. Murphy converted this into one unit by demolishing walls and building connecting bridges.

Hopper's interior initially evokes the idea of a hangar. The space is large and high, with a gigantic television screen and furniture designed by Alvar Aalto and Isamu Noguchi. Sliding walls, to which paintings can be attached, hang everywhere. Steel stairs ascend to balconies and there is a footbridge from one side of the space to the other.

Not only are the construction and furniture extraordinary, the acoustics in the house are also uncommon. It sounds like the engine room of a ship: pulsation, footsteps on iron, resonating voices, strange echoes, and the constant crackling of the intercom. As the garage doors open up to the street with a cacophony of sound, and the cars are started up in the house, the chaos seems complete.

The house and the idiosyncratic owner form a perfect match. The house also fits in with the somewhat unsavoury neighborhood. Whatever happens, the steel door will repel undesired visitors. The seclusion of the premises gives a sense of security and privacy on the inside, whereas the size and height also radiate a feeling of openness.

In his fort, Hopper feels as a fish in water. 'It looks tough,' he says simply. 'It's great.'

██████

◄ **large studio** (ground floor). The left hand panel
hangs from the ceiling and is movable, so that
the layout of the space can be altered.

▲ Painting by David Salle, chairs by Charles and
Ray Eames, and table by Isamu Noguchi.

► **inner courtyard**, which links the various buildings.

▲ **living room** Painting by Jean-Michel Basquiat.
Sofa and chairs by Alvar Aalto and low table
by Isamu Noguchi. Vases of Venetian glass
adjoin the wood stove.
▶ The large painting is by Keith Haring.
▮▶ The large painting is by Julian Schnabel.

◄ **kitchen**, on the same floor as the living room.
The female portrait is by Hopper himself, and
dates from the sixties.
► Victoria, Hopper's wife, portrayed by Julian
Schnabel.

▲ **small studio**, where various antique objects have been combined.
► **bathroom** with a glass bath and a Venetian glass dish.
I► **bedroom** Works by Hopper hang above the bed.

MARK ZEFF

globetrotter and treasure hunter

▬▬▬▬ Mark Zeff has been working as an architect and interior designer for twenty years now and always has a full agenda. He combines attractive antiques with classic twentieth-century design. In the New York world of interior designers he is one of the 'fresh guys', due to his uncluttered, untraditional approach to decorating. Film star Hilary Swank hired him because she prefers to live in a casual rather than an 'over-the-top' way.

Born in South Africa and educated in architecture and industrial design at the Royal College of Art in London, he moved to Sydney to work with Marsh Freedman Associates in building private houses and restaurants. In 1982 he went to New York to gain experience as an interior decorator. He arrived with two suitcases, one filled with clothes and the other filled with items that he had collected at flea markets and bazaars all over the world. He anticipated a short stop in the USA, but he stayed, and three years later he founded his own office.

Through the years, Zeff has managed to retain the image of being fresh, eclectic and contemporary. It is no surprise that his clientele comprises many young people who abhor a showy interior and the glamour of Hollywood. His customers are not people whose main aim is to use their interiors to make an impression on the outside world. They simply wish to realize a home where they feel comfortable and can retreat to the things to which they feel attached.

'To me, design means a blend of aesthetic feeling, knowledge and technology,' says Mark. 'These three things combined produce a certain energy.' On the basis of this vision, he easily unites English antiques with an austere industrial lamp, or French design from the forties with exotic elements. Mark points out that an interior should always be prepared to accept change. 'I regard it as the mirror of my life at a certain moment in time. If I change, my home environment also changes.'

His own house is a spacious pre-war apartment on the Upper West Side in Manhattan, with Moroccan chandeliers, mirrors, a George III desk, and austere Bibendum chairs by Eileen Gray. White walls and a dark floor form a neutral background in the living room, so that the outspoken contours of the furniture, such as the nineteenth-century Danish whitewood cabinet and the Moroccan crafted table, stand out in their full glory. The sofas and the carpet are his own designs.

The apartment itself is actually the combination of three apartments. The many corridors provide numerous corners and niches where Mark can express himself by creating amazing still lifes with the objects he collects. The whole interior is a mixture of things that don't necessarily belong together, but nevertheless harmonize beautifully.

Zeff always brings his customers home so that he can let them see how he works and how he views the world. For Hilary Swank, the acquaintance with Zeff's own apartment was decisive in commissioning him to redesign her house on Charles Street in the West Village. 'He simply generates a pleasant house, not a trophy cabinet,' according to the film star. Despite the two Oscars that she received for her roles in Million Dollar Baby and Boys Don't Cry, celebrity airs remain alien to her. She doesn't enjoy standing in the spotlight, and she avoids the gossip papers like the plague. 'I am and will always be an ordinary girl from a trailer park. A girl with a dream.'

The attitude of customers such as Swank is very dear to Mark Zeff. Despite his famous clients and the fact that he is involved in projects that are regularly the talk of the town, he remains a modest person in his work. 'I hate being associated with elitist and pricey designers,' he says. Zeff feels more like a privileged collector of beautiful objects. 'I am like a treasure hunter. A finder of absurd things I put together.'

▬▬▬▬

◄ **living room** (p. 32-33) The concave shape of the
19th-century Danish cabinet is repeated in the
two leather chairs by Eileen Gray, dating from 1929.

◄ (p. 34) Juli and Mark Zeff.

◄ (p. 36) An admirable still life, related in form:
a sculpture made by the Australian artist Dennis Allard
and a 19th-century console table that was bought
at a flea market in Nantucket.

◄ (p. 37) The sofa was designed by Zeff himself.
The table on the left comes from Morocco and the two
small round tables are by Charles and Ray Eames.
The lamps are Italian and date from the fifties.
The three photos were shot by Gianpietro Favaro, 1988.

▲ **dining room** A reflecting top was installed above a
subframe of a Le Corbusier table. The dining room chairs
are by Zeff. The elaborate mirror is French, while the lamp
comes from Morocco.

► **hall** A statue of Jeanne d'Arc from 1920,
adjoining a chair by Charles and Ray Eames.

YUSMAN & INKE

SISWANDI

Javanese tranquility amid the palm trees, rice fields and bad roads

■■■■■■ The self-designed house of Yusman Siswandi and his wife Inke is situated near the Indonesian city of Solo. The couple are part owners of the rapidly expanding BIN House empire, which has given traditional batik, the most renowned textile form of Indonesia, a modern impulse. Japan has been conquered, as have been the Middle East and America.

The Siswandis' house lies hidden among the rice fields in the outlying districts of Solo, and it is difficult for people who are unfamiliar with the region to find it. There are no signs or other indications, nor is there anyone anywhere who could possibly provide information. Moreover, the trip is further hampered by large pot-holes in the road. Palm trees and vines conceal the house from view. It only becomes evident that the destination has been reached when you are almost at the entrance.

Yusman and Inke deliberately chose this location, far removed from the heat and the noise of the big city. Nestled between the rice fields and the greenery of nature they find rest from their hectic activities for BIN House.

A stroll through the house soon explains Yusman and Inke's devotion to Indonesian craft. 'Our house hasn't been built according to established rules or one straightforward style,' say Yusman. 'It is based on tradition and the passions we nurture in our lives. We respect the past, but we certainly heed the present.'

In line with Indonesian tradition, their house has many open spaces for communal use and secluded rooms for sleeping and bathing. It is striking that the house has no modern central air-conditioning system. But due to the fact that the high rooms have windows that can be opened to allow air to flow through the house, the evening breeze in particular ensures a comfortable relief from the tropical heat. The many water features around and even in the house were not only installed because they form a part of the exceptional architecture but also because they offer cooling. Yusman and Inke have constructed attractive pools that separate the entrance pavilion from the residential wing and the detached guest accommodation. The garden behind the house accommodates the largest pool, which is only a few centimetres deep. The rear gallery, with comfortable reclining chairs, adjoins this reflecting pool. In the evenings, the pond works as an enormous mirror. Those who wish to enjoy the moon and stars at night are in their element. 'Just gaze into the water,' says Yusman. 'That's much easier than craning your neck upwards.'

The dining room and living room are situated in the middle of the house. Sunlight enters via high windows and the floors acquire an extra sheen. The living room is modern yet simple, with a mixture of antique and craft furniture, made by local manual workers. The sofas are comfortable and invite you to take a breather or to stretch out for a relaxing Indonesian pijit by a local masseur.

All the floors in the house have been paved with stones that were rescued during the demolition of an eighteenth-century house in North Java. The tiles' color matches nicely with the hand-made stones of the walls that have been constructed in a beautiful pattern. Initially, Yusman was in charge of the bricklaying activities but at

a certain moment he gave the workers free rein to realize their own artistic creations, both inside and along the pond at the rear of the house.

Good hospitality in Indonesia means that visitors are constantly spoiled with local delicacies. With the Siswandis, this occurs in the spacious dining room with a large central table, at which everyone can draw up a chair and which bears a large quantity of food that is repeatedly replenished from the adjacent kitchen. The dining room, too, is a combination of old and new. Yusman designed the lighting and had the cupboards, now full of old pots and statues from all the islands in the Indonesian archipelago, manufactured in his workplace.

Although Yusman and Inke have had no formal architectural training, they have been extremely successful in building and arranging a house in a way that was good enough to be nominated for the Aga Khan Architecture Award. To them, their family and friends, the house is primarily a comfortable place of refuge. The fact that it is isolated is an advantage, as they see it. And what about the bumps and holes in the road? Well, the prospect of a hospitable welcome and a delicious meal reduces even that discomfort to very bearable proportions.

■■■■■■

◄ **garden** (p. 44-45)) The reflecting pool behind the house.
◄ **inside/outside** (p. 47) A shallow water feature separates the
low entrance pavilion from the double-height residential area.
◄ **living room** The living room is furnished with a combination
of self-designed objects and colonial antiques.
▲ View from the living room to the guest pavilion, which is
situated next to the entrance.
► A still life with one of the hand-made shawls from Yusman
and Inke's collection.

◄ **dining room** All the furniture was designed by the residents themselves.
► Organic forms not only find a place on the table, but the staircase has
  also been designed according to the same principle.

◄ **workplace** A table bearing a Tizio with
examples of lamp designs by Yusman adjoining.
The stool for the table is also by Yusman.

▲ A focal point opposite the water feature.
The cloth has an open structure; batik was
applied to the closed parts.

► **bedroom** The simple four-poster beds, designed
by Yusman, are combined with an antique wardrobe.
Even the bed linen was made by them!

◄ **garden** The open pavilion adjoining the reflecting pool.
▲ An example of hand-made batik from the couple's collection.
► **bathroom**, with only half a roof so that the elements have free play. An unprecedented tropical experience for Westerners.

VLADIMIR KAGAN & ERICA WILSON

irresistible collector's mania in a chock-full apartment

▬▬▬ Avant-garde designer Vladimir Kagan designs sober furniture, but lives everything but a sober life. His apartment on the Upper East Side of New York is packed full with an esoteric collection of furniture, art, memories and trinkets from all over the world and especially with colorful embroidery work by his wife Erica Wilson, America's uncrowned embroidery queen and television celebrity. 'I know, I know,' Vladimir admits, 'in my work I advocate the notion of less is more. But here at home, it is always more is more.'

Those who enter this abundant apartment are overwhelmed by the magnificent display of color, and soon have the feeling that they have landed in a surprise adventure. There is something new to see and experience in every corner and behind every door. Abstract sculptures, African and Asian masks, English silver, paintings from Haiti, model trains, dried flowers, glass art, porcelain, family photos, an enormous birdcage, and no fewer than three pianos form a remarkable domestic landscape along with Erica's embroidered cushions and many furniture creations. Artistic and Bohemian: the interior is clearly a reflection of the careers of both artists and, above all, of their collector's mania.

In their work, Kagan and Wilson have been pursuing their own paths for more than fifty years. Nevertheless, they share a passion for purchasing and collecting. Vladimir even talks of 'voracious' collecting because they always return from their many trips with suitcases full of souvenirs,

and almost every day, when buying groceries, he cannot resist the urge to pick up 'something nice'.

It all began in 1955 when Erica Wilson, an Irish girl and a graduate of the Royal School of Needlework in England, came to the USA to give embroidery lessons to what she herself calls 'a group of ladies with blue blood'. She met the 28-year-old Vladimir at a party. After completing his education as an architect at Columbia University, he had taken a job in his father's furniture-making workshop in order to learn the tricks of the trade. He then had his own showroom on 57th Street. They married in Woodstock in 1957.

During the subsequent years, they both built up impressive careers. Erica had a popular program on television, published sixteen books on needlework, and ran a shop on Madison Avenue. Vladimir produced innovative furniture designs which eventually made him one of the most important furniture designers of the twentieth century.

Kagan's designs, with their bold sensual lines, raised eyebrows in the fifties, and still do to this day. More than half a century later, his distinctly contoured chairs and sofas are still regarded as 'original, contemporary and timeless', and Kagan's style icons are collected by international trendsetters such as David Bowie and Tom Ford. For celebrity designer Tom Ford, his admiration of Kagan's work was the reason, in the nineties, to furnish all the Gucci shops in the world with the Omnibus sofa that Vladimir had designed in the seventies.

In the past few years, Kagan's vintage objects have again been put back into production. The Kagans' New York apartment accommodates almost all those classic models: the living room contains the popular Omnibus sofa, and the dining room

displays the table that Kagan designed for IBM typewriters in 1957. And that is not all: there is the Fettuccine Chair from the late fifties, which was reintroduced in 1999, and Kagan's Tri-symmetric table from 1953, with a walnut subframe. Kagan nurtures a special preference for designing chairs: 'In my opinion, chairs are the designer's handwriting.'

In the thirty-five years and more that Erica and Vladimir have occupied the apartment, it has never been subjected to a facelift. When they and their three children originally took over the apartment, they painted the dining room bright orange, the hall received an intense geometric pattern in pink and red, and the bedroom walls were decorated with an English-oriented Boussac pattern. And that's the way it is today. The only thing that changes in the Kagans' house is the volume of the acquired objects and the end does not appear to be in sight. At least, as long as Wilson and Kagan maintain a travelling schedule that would exhaust a 20-year-old. 'We travel a lot and we take delight in buying. Collecting is an inspiration,' says Vladimir. 'We can't stop. We're simply addicted.'

▬▬▬

◄ **library** (p. 56-57) with the Contour Chair dating from 1953 on the left.

◄ (p. 59) A shelf of the bookcase in the library, with wooden sculptures by Vladimir's father, Illi.

▲ **living room** The rocking version of the Contour Chair, embroidered by Erica. A painting by their son Illya, an artist, rests on the easel.

► A complete mixture: a neo-Gothic cabinet combined with Kagan's Tri-symmetric table. The simple American farmstead chairs are old, while the plexiglass chair and the bent wood chair were designed by Kagan, but date from different periods. The seats were embroidered in accordance with one of Erica's designs.
The suspended lamp dates from the fifties. A glimpse of the Omnibus sofa can be obtained on the left, as well as a work by Frank Stella.

► The Corkscrew Chair, dating from 1992, with two cushions that Erica designed for the Metropolitan Museum in New York.
The large canvas is by Edward Fields.

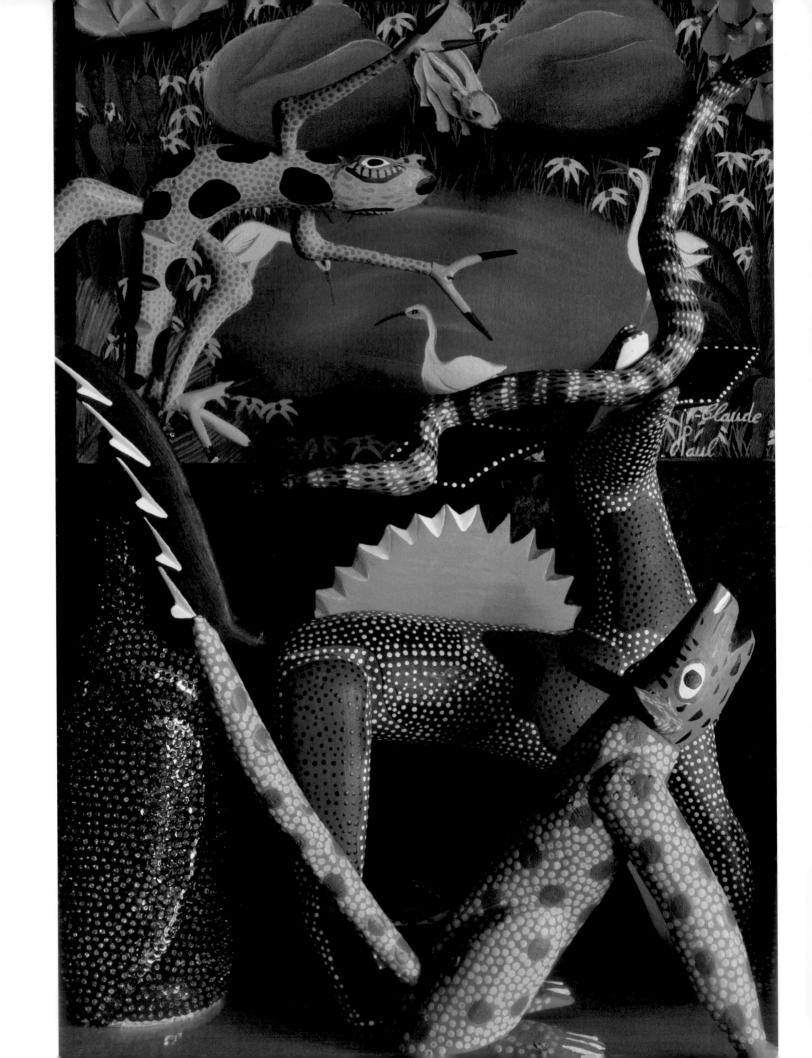

63 | VLADIMIR KAGAN & ERICA WILSON

◄ (p. 62) The Kagans have a huge collection of exotic
souvenirs, which are displayed in groups.
◄ library (p. 63) Wherever you look you are faced with
collections that are even presented in layers on the wall.
▲ bedroom The Fettuccine Chair, 1985, is on the right.
► A collection of English ceramics from the twenties
and thirties.

VLADIMIR KAGAN & ERIKA WILSON

JOHN BARMAN

eclectic is much more than simply heaping everything together

■■■■■■■ For his own personal use, successful interior architect John Barman transformed a simple beach house into a splendid country house with cosmopolitan allure. A ten-year reconstruction period witnessed the exploration of boundaries and an abandonment of traditions. 'This is what I was after,' says Barman about the result, 'a mixture of styles and materials, of modern art and outspoken furniture. Eclectic. That is the most difficult style that there is. I'm fortunate in knowing how that works.'

With his large-scale reconstruction of the beach house and its interior layout, Barman has again issued his calling card in the Hamptons and that really means something in this gold coast of New York where the super wealthy are over-represented and money alone plays no role of significance. You can only become noticed as a consequence of superior taste, vision, and nerve. Of course, this is all on the precondition that you do everything in an extremely discrete manner, because vulgar behavior is simply 'not done' in the Hamptons.

John Barman is acknowledged as one of New York's best interior designers. Strongly influenced by renowned designers from the past such as David Hicks and Billy Baldwin, Barman has now clearly developed his own style. Customers gladly choose Barman because he can translate their desires into a well-considered and tasteful concept and also because he works in various ways: occasionally color-

ful and hyper-modern, sometimes traditional and distinguished.

Barman is a true master in designing a good eclectic interior. Commenting on this talent, he says: 'The eclectic style is the most difficult style of all. It is not a matter of just heaping everything together. It's about harmony. Objects and furniture must jointly generate drama and contrast so that the interior becomes interesting, if not fascinating.'

No cost or effort is spared in the choice of furniture, upholstery and accessories. Barman will even travel to Europe to find that single special vintage smoking table by Hermes. On the other hand, he does not hesitate to shop cheaply at the popular American store Crate & Barrel. 'If it looks good, I'm satisfied.'

From his headquarters on Park Avenue in New York and a branch in Los Angeles, Barman and his team work mainly for private customers who wish to have their luxury apartment, country home or boat renovated or refurbished. Barman works with renowned architects, such as Alexander Gorlin and Preston Phillips. In collaboration with Gorlin, he converted two large apartments on New York's Upper West side into an artist's apartment annex gallery, with an extensive collection of modern America figurative art. Along with Phillips, he rebuilt an old farmstead in the Hamptons for a wealthy banker, an acquaintance of the Clintons. An enormous loft of glass and steel was added and furnished with art by Andy Warhol, vintage pieces from Hermes, and modern design by Charles Eames and Ludwig Mies van der Rohe.

In his own country house, Barman is primarily guided by tranquility, simplicity and harmony. The ambience of the beach house has remained, but it has been modernized with white walls and dark floors,

vibrant furniture, and unexpected explosions of color. The living room has various sitting areas and is large enough to throw parties. The room has a hearth and French windows that look out upon a sunken patio where the reclining chairs are waiting seductively.

What Barman initially only had in his mind for his country house has finally become reality. Along with his partner Kelly Graham, he now relishes every moment there. And that undoubtedly also applies to the guests at the parties in his renovated beach house in the Hamptons. ■■■■■■■

◄▮ **bedroom** (p. 69) Still life, a mixture of materials and periods.

▲ **living room** The chair in the foreground is French, and dates
from the forties.
The patterned chairs are vintage and come from Palm Beach.
Upholstered with an Osborne & Little fabric, they are again
completely contemporary.

▶ A bed from India functions as a table. Two classical ear chairs
flank the 19th-century French sandstone mantelpiece.

▮▶ A colored still life in which materials and periods are freely mixed.
A glimpse of the home theater can be seen through the doorway.

◄ **kitchen** The colored vases and the quirky lamp make this simple kitchen something special.

▲ **dining room** By lining up the antique dining room chairs along the wall, the dining room acquires a somewhat distinguished appearance.

The chandelier visible in the mirror was found on the street. Having been painted bright red, this lamp is now the focal point of the room.

► **home theater** The chairs in the foreground are by Paul McCobb, a renowned American furniture designer from the mid-20th century. The upholstery pattern was created by Alan Campbell in the seventies. Fashion designer Halston and Diane Vreeland of the American magazine Vogue expressed their personal approval of the collection. Quadrille has again taken the entire Campbell collection into production.

bathroom, bedroom Black/white is the most
important theme of these private rooms.
The painting above the bed was made by
Barman himself during his student days in Paris.

PETER VAN HATTUM & HAROLD SIMMONS

Villa Hertenhof: as if it has been in the family for generations

███████ In the Northwest Woods, a remote nature area on the eastern edge of the Hamptons, lies Hertenhof, a country house owned by Peter van Hattum and Harold Simmons. A former musical star and an architect, respectively, built their house according to classical American traditions. The house is brand new, but anyone who doesn't know better will think that this has been the country house of a rich aristocratic family for generations.

For more than a century, the Hamptons has been a magnet for the wealthy. It began with what is regarded as the aristocracy in America, the WASPs (White Anglo-Saxon Protestants). Those old families set the tone for the nouveau-riche Americans who had amassed a fortune within a single generation. The well-to-do who now own these luxury country homes are mainly celebrities from the worlds of film, music, fashion and nightlife.

From Manhattan, the Hamptons are a little more than two hours' drive, at least for those who manage to avoid rush hour on Friday afternoon and Sunday evening. New Yorkers are resigned to the weekend traffic jams when going to and coming from their country homes. After all, the Hamptons are really unique, due to the beautiful beaches, the sea and the dunes. Everything is still relatively unspoiled, thanks to the strict rules that apply there.

Peter and Harold do not need to take weekend traffic into account, as they have largely scaled back their working careers and spend more time in the countryside than in the city. Peter was born and raised in the Netherlands and came to the USA when the cruise ship on which he was sailing with Wim Kan's cabaret group stopped in New York on its way to a tour of the West. By chance, he heard of an audition for The Sound of Music. He gave it his best shot and landed a leading role. Having played in various Broadway productions for years, Peter began to follow another of his passions: working as an interior designer.

Harold made his mark as an architect and interior designer, and originated from the school of Albert Hadley and Sister Parish. Parish is known, among other achievements, for the fact that she assisted Jacqueline Kennedy with the restoration of the White House. The interior was stripped of the stuffy image of the fifties and transformed into the international symbol of America's good taste. Parish and Hadley worked for the absolute top of the American aristocracy: the Rockefellers, the Vanderbilts, the Astors and the Whitneys.

Harold grew up in luxury on his family's cotton plantation in Mississippi. He studied architecture at the University of Mississippi and then attended the renowned Parsons School of Design in New York. His first job was with an architectural office, and then he was employed by Parish-Hadley, where he was head of the architecture department for twenty years, his task being to design and furnish luxury houses.

In 1987, Peter and Harold founded their own firm, Van Hattum & Simmons. Their projects have been realized not only in America but also in England and South Africa. With Hertenhof, Peter and Harold have managed to realize their own dream house in the spirit of Sister Parish and Albert Hadley. Moreover, they have been inspired by classic European architecture. The country house is built on an enormous parcel of land that adjoins a nature area, meaning there are no neighbors in the vicinity. Harold and Peter's only unexpected visitors are deer and lonely hikers.

When Harold and Peter began their design activities, it was apparent to them that the outside of a house had to correspond to the inside. 'I don't particularly like entering a classic house only to discover a modern open space,' says Harold. 'I think that the style of the interior ought to harmonize with the style of the exterior.'

With the layout of Hertenhof, Peter and Harold have adhered reasonably strictly to the basic principles of the classical eighteenth-century interior. The rooms are large and high but, to avoid a feeling of being overwhelmed by the dimensions, refined use has been made of scale and proportion. The living room contains extra-large furniture that is not immediately recognizable as such. This recognition only comes when Harold points out that the occasional table in the drawing room is an English Regency table which served as a dining table for six people in their previous home. Peter and Harold are antique-lovers and many of their items have been bought during their cultural trips through Europe.

In Hertenhof, their collection of Delft pottery and Chinese porcelain has been allocated a prominent place against a backdrop of elegantly patterned wallpaper. 'A house should feel as if it has always been there,' is the view of Peter and Harold. With their antique objects, they attempt to evoke the suggestion that their interior has evolved down through the years. With Hertenhof, that aim has undeniably been achieved. If Sister Parish had been alive today, she would undoubtedly have given Harold and Peter a well-earned compliment. ███████

◄ **living room** (pp. 76-77) The mantelpiece came from a 19th-century Hudson Valley house. The painting on the mantelpiece is French and is signed: Etienne Leroux 1879. The oil painting above the grand piano comes from the Dutch Hondecoeter School. ▲ **entrance**

◄ **hall** The bust is of the French dramatist Jean de Rotrou, Chevalier de France. It is a 19th-century copy based on a 17th-century original. Original Piranesi prints adorn the wall.

◄ **living room** The chairs with the open armrests in the living room are Regency and Louis XV and still have their original embroidery. The large hand-embroidered carpet with a Regency pattern was made especially for the living room.

▲ **dining room** A pair of 19th-century papier-mâché Chinese vases flank the passage to the dining room. The walnut chairs are English: George I. The 'Jardin Chinois' wallpaper is a copy of an antique Chinese original.

dining room An antique Chinese folding screen against the wall, with Delftware accessories
from the 18th century and English chandeliers in front. Top: two Delftware plates.

◄ **library/garden room** Over the sofa is a Chinese painted scroll depicting Buddha. ▲ **bedroom** Painting by the French artist Isabelle de Ganay, 'Coucher de Soleil à la Bouille'.

ROSITA & OTTAVIO MISSONI

fifty years of Missoni
on the catwalk and at home

▬▬▬▬ To Rosita and Ottavio Missoni, the founders of the Italian fashion empire, their work is the heart and soul of their existence. World-renowned for their colorful knitwear, the Missonis have upheld their artistic vision of tradition and quality for more than fifty years. They do that on the catwalk and also in their own home.

The Missonis live and work in an eminent building in a classical nineteenth-century district of Milan. The interior reflects the cosmopolitan lifestyle of the artistic couple. Their love of modern art and architecture, and above all their exceptional sense of color, pattern and refinement, recurs in the layout and furnishings of their spacious and light apartment.

Rosita and Ottavio have been working together successfully for more than fifty years. Although they have reached the age when others may have retired, and their children Vittorio, Luca and Angela have now taken over the management of the company, the couple is still the creative impulse behind Missoni Fashion, Missoni Sport and Missoni Home.

Ottavio is the color specialist of the two ('I could have been a painter'), and Rosita is primarily the designer with unparalleled knowledge of how to produce exclusive hand-made fabrics ('I am the historical conscience of Missoni'). They enjoy experimenting with patterns and proportions. In conjunction, the Missonis have an exceptional talent for combining colors, patterns and materials in such an ingenious way

and of giving the result such luxurious allure that no one has ever successfully succeeded in copying any of Missoni's knitted products.

Rosita Jelmini and Ottavio Missoni met one another in London during the Olympic Games of 1948. Ottavio was an athlete and participated in the four hundred meter hurdles race. He came from Sicily and she from Lombardy, where her family had been engaged in producing hand-made textiles and embroideries for four generations. The couple married in 1953, five years after their first meeting, and they set up a knitting factory in Gallarate near Milan.

The early years, when they only had three knitting machines at their disposal, were somewhat lean years for the young couple. They designed woollen tracksuits for the Italian Olympic team, among others. Their real breakthrough came in 1964, when they compiled a collection in collaboration with designer Emmanuelle Kahn and displayed it during the fashion week in Milan. The collection became world news purely by accident, when Rosita decided at the last minute that the models had to remove their brassieres to avoid distorting the elegant line of the silk-knitted dresses. However, she had not realized that the dresses would become transparent under the bright spotlights. The fashion world was shocked and the news subsequently appeared in large headlines on the front pages of the newspapers.

The creativity of the Missonis also determines the ambience at home. Rosita has ensured a perfect balance between colorful and sober, austere and light-footed. The furniture, such as the sofa designed by the Italian architect Piero Pinto, one of their friends, is largely natural in color. It is the accessories and the art that lend radiant color to the Missoni home: the red chandelier above the dining table was designed by Gio Ponti for Venini (1951); the

purple stools in the hall were designed by Philippe Starck for Kartell; the painting (1929) above the bed is by Sonia Delaunay; and the wire-mesh tree in the living room is by artist Benedette Uboldini. 'Art is important for creating atmosphere,' say the Missonis. 'Art makes a house your own, and gives it soul.'

The Missoni interior remains subject to change and new objects are regularly added. 'I'm still at the age that I look forward rather than backward,' Rosita explains. It is understandable that she was initially sceptical about her daughter Angela's idea to celebrate the fiftieth anniversary with a retrospective. However, at the end of the successful fashion show she admitted, in an interview with Suzy Menkes of the International Herald Tribune, that her scepticism had vanished completely. 'I am now wildly enthusiastic. It's true: I prefer not to look back. But on the other hand: I too belong to the history of Missoni.' ▬▬▬▬

◄ **living room** (pp. 88-89 and pp. 92-93)

A pair of symmetrically arranged sideboards form a modern variation on an old theme. The sideboards were made by the Milanese sculptors Salvatore + Marie in the seventies.

The three enamel clasone objects on the left-hand sideboard were designed by Ottavio (see also p. 91).

The chandelier is by Gio Ponti for Venini (1951).

The Y Chair dining room chairs were designed by Hans Wegner (1950).

The canvas in the background displays a design for a scarf for Missoni.

The low table is by Salvatore + Marie.

The large white sofa was designed by architect Piero Pinto.

The cushions, the tablecloth, the knitted fabric draped over the chairs, and the carpet were all designed by the Missonis.

◄ **hall** (pp. 94-95)

The stained-glass window dates from 1914.

The round sofa is by Piero Pinto, the cushions by Missoni.

The two purple La Boheme stools are by Philippe Starck for Kartell.

The three drawings are by Antonio Lopez, a famous fashion illustrator who has done much work for the Missonis.

The floor was designed by Ottavio himself.

▲ **bedroom** The bedroom is much more subdued in tone than the rest of the house.

The settees with cushions come from Missoni Home.

► An embroidered panel (1929) designed by Sonia Delaunay hangs above the bed.

The bed linen is by Missoni Home.

KORTMANN

a sixth sense for space

■■■■■■ Gabriele Kortmann had definite ideas about the house of her dreams. The shiny marble, gold fittings and other ornaments she found in the house in Cologne that she had recently acquired did not appeal to her tastes. Gabriele had higher standards.

For the decoration of their previous home, Gabriele and her husband Karl Dieter had employed avant-garde architect Heinz Bienefeld. His sixth sense for space and materials appealed to them, which is why they wanted him to renovate their new house in Lindenthal – one of Cologne's better residential districts – in the same style. Initially Bienefeld was sceptical but in the end he wholeheartedly agreed to their request to turn this villa, too, into a typical Kortmann house.

They wanted an extremely modern house, designed for daring people who are not afraid of extravagant ideas. 'And I wanted lots of color,' says Gabriele, 'I had my heart set on that.' Bienefeld made a rigorous start by rearranging the spaces in the house to bring out its spatial characteristics and to create clear-cut lines throughout. The marble floor was replaced by dark wood and stainless steel. And for advice on the color spectrum, the Kortmanns consulted Heinz's son Nikolaus, who had started his career as an artist and switched to interior design when he began working for his father's firm.

Gabriele wanted color and that is what she got. Nikolaus came up with a total

concept inspired by designers and artists of De Stijl. He did not simply paint the walls but created color planes and special 3-D compositions in intense orange, salmon, aqua and other hues. The collaboration between Bienefeld senior and Bienefeld junior proved extremely fertile and created exciting and surprising sightlines in the Cologne residence. 'This house will not be to the liking of everyone,' says Bienefeld senior. 'If that were the case, we would have done something wrong.' The Kortmanns have a different opinion: 'Even visitors who do not like everything they see agree that it certainly is an extraordinary house.'

The house is more modern than appears at first glance, and this is not only caused by the contrast between the exterior and the interior, but also by the prominent modern art and furniture that Bienefeld designed specifically for the house. The Kortmanns are dedicated art lovers who own an impressive collection of works by Yves Klein, Elias Suppengrun, Yuko Shiraishi, Helmut Newton, Franz von Stuck and other renowned artists.

Are the colors on the walls perhaps too dominant? Could they cancel out the works of art or the furniture? 'On the contrary,' says Gabriele, 'contrast is something to be used, to play with. And that is what we do.' She points to the entrance hall, where the walls are painted in burgundy red that harmonizes beautifully with the large, gold painting. At the same time, the color planes also form a contrast with the bust of a ballerina and the silver service by Wilhelm Nagel on the wooden bench designed by Bienefeld.

It is not just Gabriele and her husband who feel at home in the creation of father and son Bienefeld. Their children, twins Felix and Carla-Fee, share their sentiments. Carla-Fee's favourite spot is the library, which contains her grand piano. Mother Gabriele

likes to spend time in the dining room, which she enjoys most when her guests enthuse about her house. 'We wanted a home that would not only be beautiful but where we would also feel comfortable. Of course it is a reflection of our love of modern art and architecture, but to us this house is first and foremost a place where we can recharge our batteries. Thanks to Heinz and Nikolaus Bienefeld we have a real Kortmann house again.' ■■■■■■

◄ **library** (pp. 98-99), with custom-made bookshelves and built-in cupboards.
► **entrance hall** Still life in the hall.
On the bench designed by Bienefeld, a silver tea service created in 1990 by Wilhelm Nagel.
►■ **living hall** (p. 102) A portrait by Franz von Stuck. The photograph is by Boris Becker of Düsseldorf. (p. 103) Along the walls, furniture designed by Le Corbusier.
The two chairs in the middle are Costes Chairs by Philippe Starck.
On the table, two vases by architect and designer Mendini for Venini.
dining room (p. 104) The dining room furniture was designed by Bienefeld.
The sphere is a soup tureen by Claudia Steinicke.
garden room (p. 105) Zig Zag Chair by Gerrit Rietveld.
garden room (pp. 106-107) Furniture and lamps by Heinz Bienefeld.
A Chinese horse from the Han dynasty.
On the table, a vase by Colette of Paris.
The scale model is 'Haus Macaria' in Cologne, designed by Bienefeld.

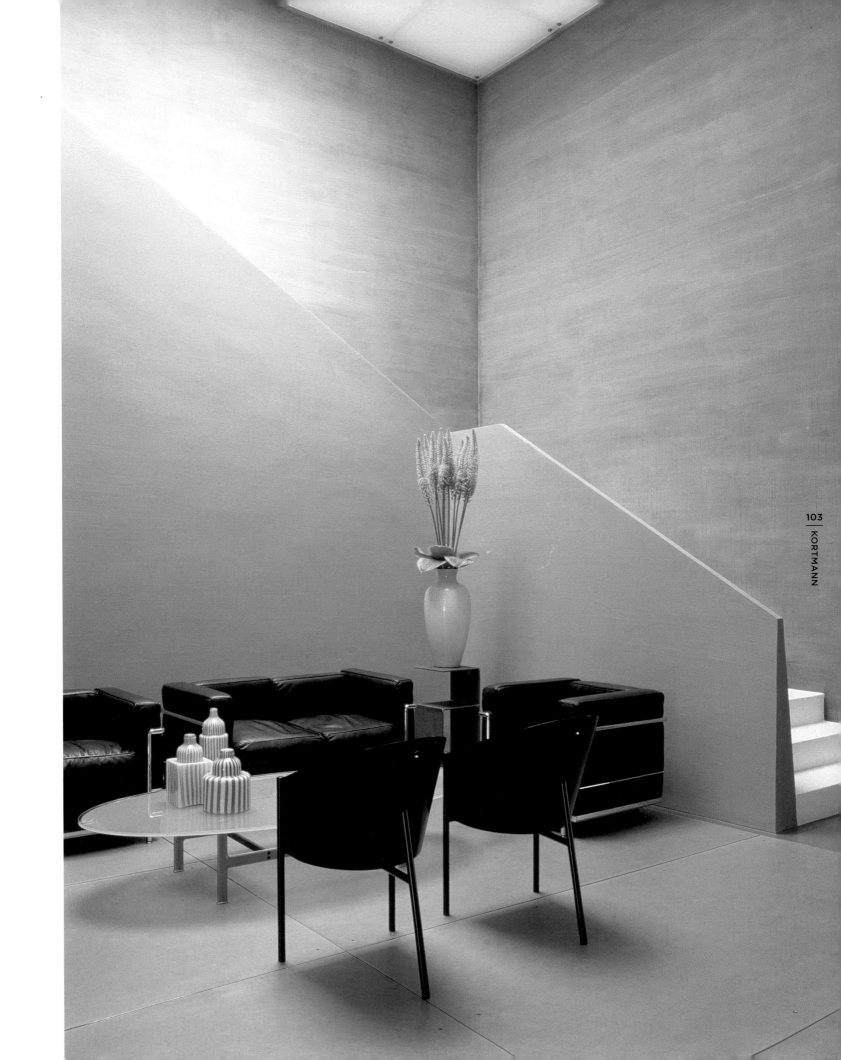

JAYA IBRAHIM

trendsetter of luxury hotels in a remote palace on Java

■■■■■■ Jaya Ibrahim is to hotels what designers like Tom Ford and John Galliano are to fashion. Ever since his collaboration with the idiosyncratic Anouska Hempel set a trend with one of the first boutique hotels, Blakes (1978), and London's first minimalist hotel, The Hempel, a few years later, Ibrahim has designed one stunning hotel interior after another. In Milan he renovated the five-star The Chedi hotel and in Miami he designed the CHI Tower apartments. At an average price of five million dollars, these come with a private swimming pool on the terrace, private butler and private jet. 'Obviously not within everyone's range,' Jaya remarks with a sense of understatement.

His huge reputation, allied to the fact that he is on the list of the world's hundred best designers published by Architectural Digest, is not simply due to the budgets at his disposal. First and foremost, Ibrahim is an innovative, high-profile designer. His style varies from modern minimalism to the theatrical and always contains exotic elements. What makes him unique is that he has the talent – based on his extensive knowledge of classical styles of architecture – to merge the traditional oriental culture of Indonesia, China and India with modern western influences. In addition, like the major trendsetters in fashion, Jaya has a keen sense of what will soon be 'hot'. He always comes up with designs that are not only unexpected but also set a new trend.

New developments are rarely immediately accepted by the masses but usually by a relatively small group of artistically inclined and fashionable people. These happy few not only want to set the trend with the clothes they wear but also with their lifestyle and they want to enjoy the very latest of everything. So, those who can afford it stay at The Chedi in Milan or buy an apartment in Miami. Not necessarily for the luxury of a terrace with a swimming pool, a private butler and so on (because these are really nothing special to these privileged individuals), but for the private mineral-water well, the Indonesian-style outdoor shower, and the exotic open-air kitchen that Jaya Ibrahim has thoughtfully created for them.

After working with Anouska Hempel in London for ten years, Jaya Ibrahim returned to his native soil on the Indonesian island of Java. To withdraw from the hectic life of travelling the globe and shaping the interiors of luxury hotels (with the associated high-flyer parties), he has settled among the rice paddies of Bogor in the north of Java. Simply dressed in sarong and wearing slippers, he feels his new life evokes the calm pace of life of the colonial days, far removed from anything to do with the jet set.

The sloping rice paddies of Bogor form the backdrop to Jaya's country house, which he originally built for his father and his mother, a princess from an ancient Javanese dynasty. The mansion, which is called Cipicung, has the dimensions of a palace and overlooks the majestic Mount Salak, one of Java's volcanoes. In many ways, Cipicung resembles a large colonial villa but it is also reminiscent of a Grecian temple. The garden brings the gardens of Versailles to mind, due to the many obelisks that Ibrahim has situated in the grounds to mark sightlines. He designed the palace in accordance with the principles of classical architecture as laid down by the Italian Renaissance architect Andrea Palladio. Symmetry, proportion and scale are central to these principles and Ibrahim has carried the concept through to the last detail.

The main building and two visitors' wings are situated around patios studded with palms higher than the buildings themselves. The trees echo the form of a classical Javanese roof on stilts: the pendopo, a building type frequently used in Javanese palace architecture. The private rooms are at the back of the palace; the public rooms are at the front. The stately dining room, located between the steps and the living room, forms the heart of the palace. All rooms run into each other and thus form long corridors across the house. It has a roofed porch that provides shelter both during the day when the scorching sun is high and after sunset when the tropical heat has been replaced by a sultry temperature.

The stark colonial furniture and many batiks create an old-fashioned and even somewhat spartan look. But the beautiful still lifes and ingenious combinations of textiles, paintings and objects on the walls give the rooms a modern, understated elegance with an undertone of grandeur. Jaya Ibrahim is not interested in what people believe to be his style. With Cipicung, he aimed for an exterior and interior ambience that would fit harmoniously with the Bogor landscape of rice fields, both now and in the future. 'To me,' states Jaya, 'this meant that I had to seek a balance between the modern western world and oriental cultures.' Ibrahim added an aristocratic whiff to Javanese spirituality. After all, Cipicung is a palace, and he the son of a princess. ■■■■■■

◀ı **front garden** (pp. 108-109) The front garden is separated
from the paddies lower down by a sharply outlined
U-shaped pond. From the terrace, the garden seems
to merge smoothly with the adjoining landscape.

◀ı (p. 110) Jaya in front of the palace façade.

◀ı **courtyard** (p. 111) with a view into the study with its
Venetian façade: one of the sightlines that connects
the palace interior with the landscape outside.

◀ı **study** The table and chairs were designed by Jaya.

◀ **living room** The living room contains a mix of furniture
and lamps designed by Jaya and colonial objects.
Vintage family photographs adorn the wall.

◄ı **kitchen** The detached worktable is a good example
of how an ultra-clean design can still blend in with
a traditional environment.
▲ **veranda** Breakfast on the veranda includes a view
of Mount Salak in the distance.
◄ **dining room** All the furniture was specially designed
for this room.

◄ bathroom
▲ bedroom

MICHELE OKA DONER

a beachcomber in a loft in New York

Michele Oka Doner looks like a ballerina. But the straight white gown also makes her resemble a high priestess. She is a woman with a clear signature and a woman who, with feminine grace, has breathed new life into a sense of nature.

Michele Oka Doner is about to become an American icon in the tradition of Georgia O'Keeffe and Louise Nevelson. O'Keeffe was mainly known for her surreal paintings with flowers and skeletons. Louise Nevelson made her reputation with her sculptural walls: large, free-standing wooden boxes filled with smaller boxes and geometric pieces of wood, driftwood, small wheels and buttons.

Michele's artistic reworking of 'A Walk on the Beach' has become a large-scale project at Miami's International Airport. She had more than two thousand bronze 'treasures from the sea' set into the floor and she will probably be invited to decorate thousands of square yards in another of the airport's terminals in the same vein.

Michele moved into the loft in Lower Manhattan (part of a derelict factory) in 1985, after looking at more than eighty pieces of real estate in New York that did not provide what she was after: a place where she and her husband Fred Doner could raise their two sons. Although the sons have now grown up and live elsewhere, the layout of the loft has remained the same. It is still a single open space with screened-off sections and low walls, where you only have to lift your head to make contact with all those present. The former boys' rooms on the mezzanine have a low partitioning wall across which the ground floor can be seen, where life seems to be that of the market place.

The divided spaces are now occupied by Michele's sculptures, with some exceptions, such as the area where a chair by Carlo Bugatti has been strategically placed. In the 1940s, this scion of the famous Italian car dynasty created furniture inspired by Africa. For the rest, Michele's art can be found all over the place. Photographs, dried leaves, driftwood and tools adorn the walls of her studio, while the kitchen contains a silver vase and a silver platter in the shape of huge rolled-up leaves.

Under the stairs by a Japanese artist we find the exotic Coral/Wave Chair (1993) made of silver after a design by Michele. She also designed the round bronze bench in the center of the space, on which books and magazines combine with mounds of dried leaves to form a seemingly random composition. Some bronze objects that are finished and ready to become part of the new 'A Walk on the Beach'-project lie on the floor near the circular bench.

In the meantime she is preparing a new exhibition of bronzes in the Marlborough Gallery and has been invited by the Frederik Meijer Gardens and Sculpture Park in Grand Rapids to decorate a floor with a surface area of 150,000 square feet. She will also be flying to Munich shortly to design statuettes for the prestigious Nymphenburg porcelain factory. Michele Oka Doner has many new projects and challenges, and her admirers have much more to look forward to. ▬▬▬▬

▬▬▬▬▬ Her family expected her to become a biologist, but she chose to be an artist instead. In her New York loft that once served as a location for the film Ghost starring Demi Moore and Patrick Swayze, Michele Oka Doner works on her fascinating sculptures, which command a premium in the marketplace. She also lives in this tall space – with a ceiling height of 20 feet – which has no doors but does have screened-off spaces for sleeping, reading and relaxing.

Corals, shells, driftwood and other natural materials form both the inspiration for her art and its constituent elements. The 'New York Beachcomber' shows her work at the elite Marlborough Gallery, designs glassware for Steuben and creates silver objects for Christofle. 'There aren't too many people who walk along the beach with a magnifying glass and scrutinize everything that drifts ashore. But I do. And I love it,' she explains.

Michele grew up in sunny Florida, where her father was twice elected mayor of Miami Beach. When she was young, she could often be found on the beach, where she collected shells, pieces of coral, driftwood, leaves, algae and seeds. Her family expected her to study Biology, but Michele preferred to do something creative with her fascination for these objects washed up by the sea. She decided to become an artist.

With her classic profile and dark hair, which she has drawn back into a tight knot,

◄ı (pp. 118-119) The modern architecture forms a stark contrast with the loft architecture of a button factory built in 1815 and Michele's organic work as exemplified by the free-standing bronzes of human figures (from left to right: 'Sargossum', 'Radiant Figure', 'Colossus' and 'Tempest', 2003).

◄ı (p. 120) Michele carrying Divining Fork, a 'burning bush' sculpture.

◄ı (p. 121) The bronze bench – 'Ice Ring Bench', 1990 – was designed by Michele. On the floor, bronze and ceramic shapes to be incorporated in architectural projects.

◄ı **living space** (p. 122) In the foreground, the Coral/Wave Chair, cast in silver in 1993.
The space behind the stairs is the TV room.

◄ı (p. 123) A bench that is one of a suite of furniture designed by Carlo Bugatti.
The suite was part of the estate of Andy Warhol. The Celestial Chair from 1987 has a similar motif as the Totem Stool from 1990, also on this page. Both were designed by Michele.

◄ **studio** A prototype of a bronze gilt door and a collection of sculptures Michele created between 1965 and 1980.

▼ 'Tempest', a human bronze statue; on the floor, red wax figures, ready to be cast in bronze.

► work shed, where the red wax is heated and shaped, with storage facility for blueprints below the ceiling and a huge collection of beach finds.

ı► studio (p. 126) with a plan for 'A Walk On The Beach' in the North Terminal of Miami International Airport in the background.

ı► **kitchen** (p. 127) The detached kitchen unit resembles a modern sculpture. Many of the family's heirloom serving pieces have found a place in the kitchen. The vase and large silver leaf were made by Michele.

LEVINAS

old villa is the trendiest home in Washington, DC

███████ Do not be fooled by the classic façade covered in white plaster and the green shutters: the stately villa owned by Argentinian art collectors Daniël and Mirella Levinas is probably the trendiest home in the whole of Washington, DC. Behind the façade, the entire interior has become ultramodern after a spectacular renovation by Salo Levinas (brother and brother-in-law of the owners).

Before moving in, the Levinas lived in a New York loft, but they immediately fell in love with this 1840 monument built in Georgetown, the fashionable district where Pamela Harriman and Jacqueline Kennedy once gave their soirées. The mansion used to belong to Evalyn Walsh McLean, the one-time owner of the Hope Diamond. With the arrival of the Levinas, the conversations behind the green shutters no longer concern legendary gems but world-class modern art.

When Daniël and Mirella bought the mansion, they immediately called in their brother Salo. Salo Levinas was born and trained in Argentina and has been working successfully for more than twenty years as an architect and furniture designer in his native country and in the USA. The conversion of the Washington villa took a lot of time and effort. The town council of Old Georgetown and the U.S. Commission of Fine Arts needed seven months to approve the renovation. 'They demanded that, from the outside, everything should look the same as it had always been,' explains Salo. 'That was not simple, but we succeeded in the end.' In contrast to the strict rules governing changes to the villa's exterior, Levinas could do what he liked with the interior. This gave him the opportunity to take drastic action. The old-fashioned Georgetown rooms were converted into clean-lined spaces that not only provide the occupants with spacious and comfortable living areas but, most of all, do justice to the works of art in them.

Salo opted for floors in white terrazzo and dark wenge to serve as a neutral backdrop for the modern furniture and the lively art of Matthew Barney, Anish Kapoor and countless other artists. Particularly the conspicuous high space has been given all the characteristics of a top museum. Half of the space is reserved for art; the other half for living. 'I like to keep heights under control in all situations. Otherwise, people will feel uncomfortable,' Salo explains, while pointing to the built-in cupboards and bookshelves. He included the huge glass sliding doors to optically lengthen the space.

The doors of the living room open up to a terrace with swimming pool; the gallery doors give access to a small garden. The terrazzo floor and austere pergola of stainless steel and aluminium give the terrace and swimming pool a clean, modern look.

The Levinas are not only surrounded by art, they also sit on it. In the living room, a rectangular sofa by Baron & Baron forms an ensemble with Poul Kjaerholm's Pk 22 chairs. The famous Egg Chair in orange was given a place in the library, with a piece by Andy Warhol, while the dining room sports the classic BRNO chairs of Ludwig Mies van der Rohe. 'Colors and textures are essential elements in a modern house like this,' Levinas believes. 'Otherwise, it becomes dull.'

The impact of light is important in this mansion full of art. Electrically control-led roller blinds ensure that the light is softened to protect the works of art from overly bright sunlight. Much attention has been paid to artificial lighting too: fluorescent and halogen light fixtures in sophisticated combinations have been all but concealed in the walls.

The Levinas set great store by the placement and hanging of the works, and consulted none other than Olga Viso, the director of the Hirshhorn Museum and Sculpture Garden. They had all pieces photographed and had these photographs placed in a scale model of the house before making the final arrangements. The art lovers did not call in expert help to place their furniture. This they did themselves. 'After all, this is not an art gallery,' they explain. 'This is a home containing art.' ███████

◄▮ **staircase** (p. 131) On the left, a work by
Maria Fernanda Cardosa.
Behind the stairs, a glimpse of the dining room.
◄▮ **living room** Round sculpture Bascules by
Rubens Mano. Sofa by Baron & Baron.
◄ The fiberglass hare is by Regerio Degaki.
The work above the hearth is a Massimo Vitali;
to its right, a work by Cilde Miereles.

kitchen

breakfast corner with Tulip table and chairs by
Eero Saarinen, 1955-1956.

dining room with BRNO chairs by Ludwig Mies van der Rohe.
A sculpture by Valeska Soarez is draped over the railing;
on the wall, a Vik Muniz.

library The orange work was made by Brazilian artist Beatriz Milhazes.
The drawing of Mao was made by Andy Warhol.
The Egg Chair is by Arne Jacobsen.

▲ **bedroom** with art video Love by Rivane
Neuenschwander playing.
The photographs on the wall are by Jaroslav Rossler.
The chair is by Charles and Ray Eames.
◄ **bathroom** The bath and washstand are by Agape.
On the washbasin, a statue by d'Urs Fisher.

ROBERT

COUTURIER

savoir-faire
to the last detail

▬▬▬ Robert Couturier lives up to his name: he is the couturier among interior designers. Haute couture, that is, because Couturier only settles for the very best. He furnishes houses with the finest antiques, the best art and the most precious fabrics. As Dior and Chanel create dresses, so he creates interiors.

Couturier was born in Paris, but now lives and works in New York. His childhood, being raised by his grandmother in a 16th arrondissement house designed by Jean Michel Frank (that urban environment was softened with time spent in her French country side house and mountain retreat), clearly left its mark on his sensibilities for design. His approach has been described as dramatic, stylish and opulent. He loves historical interiors, French design of the 1940s, and hand-embroidered fabrics by François Lesage (the Parisian embroidery house of French haute couture). He is creating interiors that have a historic reference point, yet are infused with the essence of today. He loves, for example, to take classic patterns out of context or blow them up to give them a modern look. 'I adore the patterns of the French eighteenth century,' he says, 'but I never use them in their original state because I don't like to rewrite history. After all, we don't live in the eighteenth century. We live now.'

Linkages between pieces is also a factor that Couturier recognizes when designing an interior. 'I enjoy playing what I call the game of associations, which has no rules,' he says when asked about how he knows what to combine. That linkage can be simplicity versus complexity, quality as an overriding factor, or historic ancestry. It quickly becomes obvious that intellect plays as much a part in his decorating approach as does an innate aesthetic sense.

Couturier believes that an interior is not only designed for a customer, but also about a customer. His narrative decorating is designed, not to tell a story about him, but to convey the spirit of the owners. It becomes a visage that illustrates the underlying unique personality of the owner; he attempts to convey that personality by illustrating with decoration the inner life of the client. 'I am also a bit extravagant,' the maestro himself explains. 'I build a setting for my clients. Some reproach me for doing this, but I consider such a reproof as a compliment, since it is not just what I do; it is also, in my opinion, the correct thing to do. After all, people who furnish their homes show who they are and put their life and philosophy of life into the limelight.'

Although Couturier is mainly employed by the super rich, many of whom are French and American tycoons like Princess Wolkonsky and Anne Hearst, he also has a younger and slightly less wealthy clientele who love to work with him. The Americans feel that Couturier has a loose French style, while the French find his approach rigorously American. Be that as it may, quality and a personal touch are important principles that guide Couturier in his interior design. He is so discerning that he always aims for museum quality when selecting antiques. 'Top quality is the basis for success,' he states. He abhors imitation and he cares nothing for the latest trend that mixes art with kitsch. 'Although this may be refreshing,' he admits, 'it is not to my taste. Peaceful coexistence can only go so far.'

He regularly travels to Europe, where he spends much time visiting antique shops, markets and art galleries. Couturier writes down everything he finds of interest and later files his notes. On his journeys, he has found unique pieces for his own apartment, such as a Louis XVI dining table, two eighteenth-century Chinese bookcases and an antique Japanese mirror, for example. The pièce de resistance is the wrought-iron sofa created by Adnet in 1940. On the walls, twentieth-century art: a tapestry by Fernand Léger and a photograph of Casa Malaparte. With the eye-catching lamps of Paulin Paris and the hand-embroidered curtains and bedspread by Lesage thrown into the mix, the atmosphere of the apartment is pleasant and elegant.

'Never forget the past,' Couturier finally emphasizes. He believes that heirlooms and other personal items are essential elements of an interior. 'I am shocked when clients tell me they want everything to be new. Why should you want that? Everybody needs memories. Always ensure, therefore, that you are close to objects from a previous life.' ▬▬▬

living room The table is an original
designed by Adnet; the legs are
decorated with porcelain figures.
The lamp is also French forties
and designed by Jean Perzel.
The sculpture on the table, a bull
ridden by a mermaid, was made
by the son of Gauguin.

living room (see also pp. 138-139) On the left, a sofa with a zebra-print cover by Adnet from the forties, French. In front of it, an African stool. The white settee is Louis XVI. On the wall, a photograph of Casa Malaparte by François Hallard.

living room The rug is a 19th-century carpet from Persia but with obvious Chinese influences.
The two white chairs are replicas of an original from the forties. A tapestry by Léger hangs above a wrought iron sofa by Adnet.

146

bathroom

bedroom The mural and the two light sculptures in the form of busts on golden pillars are by Paulin Paris. The bedspread was embroidered by Atelier Lesage.
On the wall, a photograph of Casa Malaparte by François Hallard. On the left, an American wrought-iron chair from the forties and a French chest of drawers from the early 18th century.

POTL
THE PEOPLE OF THE LABYRINTHS

the art hoards of
The People of the Labyrinths

They love color and are expressive: Dutch fashion designers Geert de Rooij and Hans Demoed of The People of the Labyrinths. There was a time when they designed costumes for large ballets and operas in Amsterdam. The theatrical and colorful features so characteristic of the style of the fashion collections of The People of the Labyrinths can also be found in their own home: an amazing world brimming with art objects and collections.

Geert and Hans live in a town house on a hill top in a green suburb of the city of Arnhem. They bought the villa, built in 1902, on the recommendation of their good friend, photographer Erwin Olaf. A thorough renovation was in order before they could move in. The previous owner, a large firm of architects, had covered up ceilings and fireplaces and poured concrete on the floors. The house was virtually uninhabitable. As much as possible, Geert and Hans have restored all the original elements – such as the Jugendstil decorations and the Mechlin panelling from the 1920s for example – to their former glory.

When they had finished their fashion design studies at the Arnhem academy, Geert and Hans had no idea about the career they wished to pursue. The first step towards a joint future was taken when they were asked to show a collection to precede a Karl Lagerfeld show. 'People liked what they saw. And then the ball started rolling.' Now they not only design clothes but also furniture, interior fabrics,

rugs and glassware. They have launched a perfume line, published a book on 22 years of The People of the Labyrinths, opened their own shops in Amsterdam, Antwerp and Moscow and have sales outlets all over the world. Celebrities such as Liz Taylor, Cher and the Rolling Stones have been wearing their outfits for years and younger stars in trendy Hollywood are also discovering the unique designs of The People of the Labyrinths.

The two designers accept the fact that they are better known abroad than in their own country. 'That has really always been the case,' Hans states resignedly. 'Perhaps it is because we do not belong to the Amsterdam fashion in-crowd and are reluctant to put ourselves into the limelight. But it may also be that our style is too expressive for the Netherlands.'

In keeping with the style of The People of the Labyrinths, the Arnhem villa where Hans and Geert live is slightly eccentric. Interesting objects stand, lie and hang everywhere: from glassware to china, from art books to photographs and paintings. These varied objects are bound into a living whole by furniture, fabrics and accessories from their own collection, with the colors harmoniously blending into each other. According to Hans, Geert is the avid collector. He says that he personally prefers a calm, empty interior but that Geert cannot resist taking home new finds all the time. 'A vase, a plate, a paperweight. Sometimes a piece of art and the next time a kitschy souvenir and before you know it, a new collection is born.'

The villa is so large that it forms a labyrinth in which someone unfamiliar with the territory may easily get lost. The ground floor houses the dining room, study and reception room, as well as the kitchen and the main library with art and photo books. The first floor, where once forty architects worked, contains the spacious bedroom,

an ample bathroom, a study and a smaller library. The top floor, which can also be reached by a flight of stairs from the bedroom, houses the extensive wardrobe of Hans and Geert and provides accommodation for guests.

Another striking feature of the house is the huge amount of art it contains. Countless paintings, sketches, collages and photographs cover the walls, while many glass and china still lifes adorn tables, sideboards and cupboards. There are works by Erwin Olaf, Bettina Rheims and Anya Janssen, each a favorite artist and personal friend of Geert and Hans. A cabinet they designed themselves harmoniously accommodates such varied items as objects by Borek Sipek, Wedgwood tableware, Chinese porcelain and Delftware souvenirs. And the same goes for the collection of Buddhas and paperweights on a wooden altar from Belgium.

Hans and Geert see their house as more than just a place where they can relax and receive guests: it is also a place of work. They love to create new designs in their own labyrinth. Now that they own a shop in Amsterdam, they visit the capital more often, but they will not even contemplate ever leaving the town of Arnhem. 'Our life here is perfect. We enjoy the peace and quiet. We are busy enough with our work as it is. And The People of the Labyrinths brings the whole world into our home anyway. What more do we want...'

◄◄ **main library** (pp. 148-149). On the left, a work by
Kahn and Selesnick. Above the secretary, photographs
by Leni Riefenstahl. On the floor, a work by Erwin Olaf.

▲ **living room** Furniture from their own POTL collection.
On the wall (top to bottom) works by: Anya Janssen,
Mark Wayland ('Aiden') and Erwin Olaf.

▶ The large piece on the left is 'Inri' by Bettina Rheims.

▶ Glassware by Boris Sipek.

▶ A chair by POTL, a painting by Anya Janssen behind it.

▶ **small library**, with furniture by POTL.

▲ **kitchen** The chandelier is by Boris Sipek.

▶ **dining room** Chairs by Charles and Ray Eames, table by
POTL, and on the wall works of several photographers,
among them Duane Michaels and Wouter de Ruyter.

▲ **bedroom** The large painting is by Anya Janssen,
the garden gnome is by Philippe Starck and the
furniture is by POTL.

▶ **dressing room**

▮▶ **bathroom**

▲ **study** with a portrait of Mick Jagger by Andy Warhol.
The photograph was made by Jack Pierson.
▶ **main library** with furniture by POTL.
▷ **landing** The work of art is by Roelof Mulder.
The armchairs are part of the POTL collection.

THE PEOPLE OF THE LABYRINTHS